P9-BJB-756

DESERT TREK

Library of Congress Cataloging-in-Publication Data
Milner, Cedric.
    Desert trek.
    (Young explorers)
    Bibliography: p.
    Includes index.
    Summary: Explores the dry, sandy environment of the desert, uncovering the mysteries of
plants and animals that hoard water to ensure survival during the driest times of the year.
    1. Deserts--Juvenile literature. [1. Deserts] I. Johnson, Paul, 1951-   ill. II. Title. III. Series:
Young explorers (Milwaukee, Wis.)
GB612.M55   1988   508.315'4   88-42906
ISBN 1-55532-919-5 (lib. bdg.)

North American edition first published in 1989 by

Gareth Stevens Children's Books
7317 West Green Tree Road
Milwaukee, Wisconsin 53223, USA

US edition copyright © 1989. First published in the United Kingdom with
an original text copyright © 1989 Victoria House Publishing Ltd.

All rights reserved. No part of this book may be reproduced or used in any
form or by any means without permission in writing from Gareth Stevens, Inc.

Series editor: Valerie Weber
Research editor: Scott Enk
Cover design: Laurie Shock

1 2 3 4 5 6 7 8 9 94 93 92 91 90 89

YOUNG EXPLORERS

DESERT TREK

Written by Prof. C. Milner
Illustrated by Paul Johnson

CONTENTS

Gareth Stevens Children's Books • Milwaukee

DESERT PROFILE

There are deserts in Africa, Asia, Australia, South and North America, and even Antarctica. In fact, more than a third of the Earth's land surface is desert or desertlike. In most desert areas, less than 10 inches (25 cm) of rain falls each year. The temperature is hot during the day and much colder at night.

Most people imagine sand dunes when they think of deserts, but there are also stony, salty, mountainous, and flat deserts.

Some areas are dry because they are far away from the sea. They get none of the moisture that sea winds normally carry over land. Other areas are dry because they are in the rain shadow of a mountain range. When winds and clouds pass over high mountains, they drop most of the moisture they contain so the land on the other side of the range may get little or no rain.

North Africa's Sahara is the world's largest desert, covering an area almost as big as the United States.

The Sahara has fierce sandstorms and dangerous creatures. Learn more about dangers like this on p. 12.

Most of central Australia is a desert plain called the Outback. Rock formations rise above this plain. One example is Ayers Rock, famous for its ancient Aboriginal paintings.

Like most deserts, the Outback is rich in wildlife. Unique animals like the kangaroo and the thorny devil are plentiful. Find out more about desert animals on pp. 14-19.

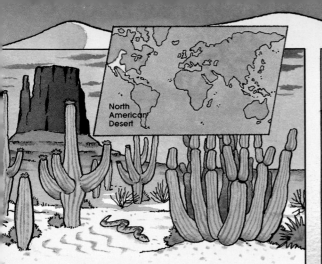

North American deserts, you can see some fascinating animals and plants. For example, you might find a cactus 50 feet (15 m) high (see p. 20), see the strange tracks of a side-winding snake (see p. 16), or hear the warning rattle of the deadly diamondback rattlesnake (see p. 12).

There are many smaller deserts. They include the Gobi Desert in Mongolia, the Atacama Desert in Chile, the Kalahari in southern Africa, and the desolate Arabian Desert, first crossed by Wilfred Thesiger in the late 1940s. You can find out more about desert explorers on p. 6.

Hunter-gatherers

Nomads

People live in the desert in two different ways. In some regions, people are nomadic. They move from place to place in search of grazing for their animals. In other regions, the people are hunter-gatherers, hunting animals and gathering plants for food. You can find out more about both ways of living on pp. 22-25.

DESERT EXPLORERS

If you visit a desert, don't make the mistake of thinking you are the first person ever to go there. It's likely that previous visitors have been there before and that you and your expedition could use their experiences. You should read their accounts and talk to local people, who have probably done some exploring themselves without writing it down. Some of the most remarkable desert journeys are described below.

Arabia has some of the harshest desert country in the world, and the Empty Quarter, between the Persian Gulf and the Gulf of Aden, is the most barren area of all, a sea of sand with huge dunes up to 790 feet (240 m) high. Wilfred Thesiger became the first European to cross the eastern end in the late 1940s along with his Bedouin companions. They journeyed over 1,000 miles (1,600 km) of unmapped desert by camel.

The first Australian settlers to venture into the Outback w nineteenth-century explore search of fabled lakes, gold and grazing land for anima

In 1844, a group led by Charles Sturt set out from Adelaide to look for a huge lake thought to be in the center of the continent. The took bullocks, 200 sheep, an even a boat.

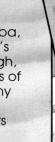

Thesiger's main barrier was the Uruq Al Shaiba, a huge wall of sand. Al Auf, the expedition's head guide, managed to find a way through, and finally the expedition reached the oasis of Dhafar to complete their epic journey. If any of their camels had died, or if their water supply had run out, the expedition members would certainly have died.

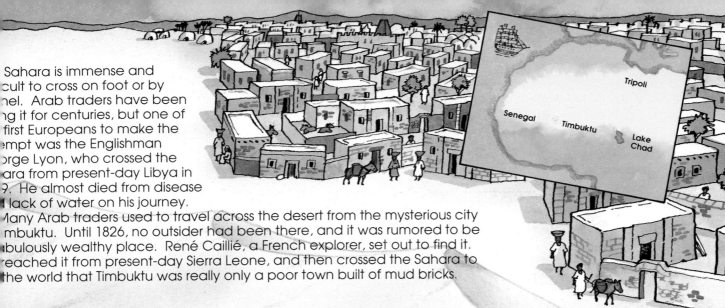

Sahara is immense and
cult to cross on foot or by
nel. Arab traders have been
ng it for centuries, but one of
first Europeans to make the
empt was the Englishman
orge Lyon, who crossed the
ara from present-day Libya in
9. He almost died from disease
lack of water on his journey.
Many Arab traders used to travel across the desert from the mysterious city
mbuktu. Until 1826, no outsider had been there, and it was rumored to be
bulously wealthy place. René Caillié, a French explorer, set out to find it.
eached it from present-day Sierra Leone, and then crossed the Sahara to
he world that Timbuktu was really only a poor town built of mud bricks.

Despite heat, drought, and illness, the explorers crossed a desert which they named after Sturt. They traveled as far as the southern edge of the Simpson Desert before they had to turn back.

In 1860, a large reward was offered to the first person who could cross Australia from south to north. A group led by Robert Burke succeeded first, but only one man survived their return journey.

A group led by John Stuart also crossed the continent. His expedition survived, but Stuart himself was half-blind by the time his party staggered into the town of Adelaide.

In 1850, Heinrich Barth, James Richardson, and others began an amazing journey of over 3,000 miles (4,800 km) across the Sahara. Richardson died on the journey, but Barth continued to Timbuktu and Lake Chad. He also made valuable drawings of the plants and animals he found.

Early desert explorers were very brave, but they made many mistakes that cost some of them their lives. With the right planning and equipment, no one needs to risk his or her life on a desert journey today.

EQUIPMENT LIST

Deserts are dangerous places. If you go on a desert expedition, it's crucial that you take the right equipment. It could save your life!

To travel to desert countries, you usually need a passport and certificates to show that you have been vaccinated against illnesses such as yellow fever and malaria, diseases carried by mosquitoes.

You must take radio equipment to keep in regular contact with people who could rescue you in an emergency.

You must take a snakebite kit, including devices to remove the poison in case you are bitten. However, you should try to get medical help first and only use your kit as a last resort. Never try to suck the poison out — it could kill you!

Take knapsacks for your equipment. Pack everything inside plastic bags to keep out dust and sand.

If you bring a camera and film, you must keep them cold. If you are camping in one place, bury them to keep them cool.

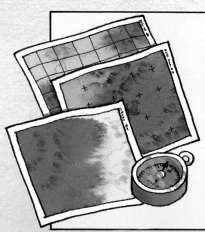

You will need a compass and some satellite pictures or aerial photos. They will tell you much more than ordinary desert maps that can become outdated in a short time.

It will be helpful to future desert travelers if you make your own maps and write notes about the areas you travel through.

In the desert, sand and rocks reflect the Sun' rays, increasing the desert temperature. To keep cool and to protect yourself from sunb wear loose-fitting cotton clothes that cover as much as possible, like a long-sleeved shirt long trousers, and a wide-brimmed hat.

You must put sunscreen lotion on exposed skin. Make sure your feet stay comfortable b wearing thick cotton socks and lightweight, sturdy, trekking boots.

If you are traveling by car or Range Rover, you must be careful not to get stuck in soft sand. If you do, you will have to dig your way out, using boards to help the vehicle's wheels get a grip on the sand.

Alternatively, you could travel by camel, but if you hire camels, you should also hire their drivers because camels can be difficult to handle.

Water is crucial to your survival in the desert. You may need at least three gallons (11 liters) a day.

You can never rely on maps to find where the water is — it may be contaminated or dried up! You must carry your supply with you in plastic bottles, checking them daily to make sure you have enough for your journey. Learn about ways of finding water in the desert on p. 10.

...eserts can be very cold at night, with ...mperatures sometimes going below the ...eezing point, so you need a high-quality ...eeping bag to keep you warm. You could ...ther use a tent or sleep outside. It's better ... avoid sleeping on the ground if possible in ...ase a snake or a scorpion crawls in with you ... keep itself warm! A hammock is useful if ...ere are any trees, or you could use a cot ... keep you off the ground.

It is a good idea to pack an unbreakable metal mirror to use as a last-ditch way of contacting possible rescuers.

If you hold the mirror toward the Sun and move it around, it will flash brightly. Because the desert air is normally still and the land-scape is often flat and bare, this light signal may be visible for many miles.

DESERT SURVIVAL

You must study and plan for the dangers you might encounter to survive in the desert. Here are some common expedition problems and travel rules.

There is one rule above all others in the desert — always know where your next drink of water is coming from. You should always carry enough water to last until you reach your next known supply, and you must check your water supply regularly. Remember, you can never rely on maps to find water sources.

If you run out of water supplies, you must try to conserve the water in your body until you reach a new source. You can cut down on sweating by traveling only at night and by resting in the shade during the day.

If you have some water that is unfit to drink, you could use it to wet your clothes to help reduce the water evaporating from your body.

To get emergency water, you could dig a well where there might be a supply — for example, in a dry streambed. You could try to get a small amount by building a desert still, which works on the principle that even in the driest deserts, there is moisture deep in the soil.

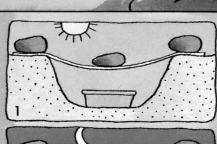

To make a still, you must dig a hole and put a bucket in the bottom. Cover the hole with plastic wrap and seal the edges with rocks. When the temperature drops at night, the soil surface will get cold, but the soil down in the hole will stay warm. The plastic wrap will get cold, and the water from the soil beneath will condense on the underside of the plastic and run into the bucket.

You can drown in the desert! careful not to sleep in dry rive beds, because rain from man miles away can suddenly floo the riverbed, turning it into a raging torrent of water.

You should always be care when crossing a flowing river Riverbeds that run through sa change depth quickly, and y may find the water much dee than you expected.

People often think it is easy to get water from desert cacti. While some cacti do hold water in their spongy tissue (see p. 20), it is difficult to extract and can taste unpleasant.

In the Kalahari Desert of southern Africa, the San tribespeople know where to look for plant roots, called tubers, that contain water. But a person cannot survive on only this liquid.

If you expect rescuers to search for you, there are a few rules that you must follow. If you have a vehicle, stay with it — rescuers can see the vehicle more easily from the air. It will also provide shade and some water from its cooling system.

If you cannot make radio contact, you could use a mirror to signal to search parties (see p. 9). If you see an airplane, flash the mirror at the pilot and arrange rocks or clothes in obvious shapes such as an "X."

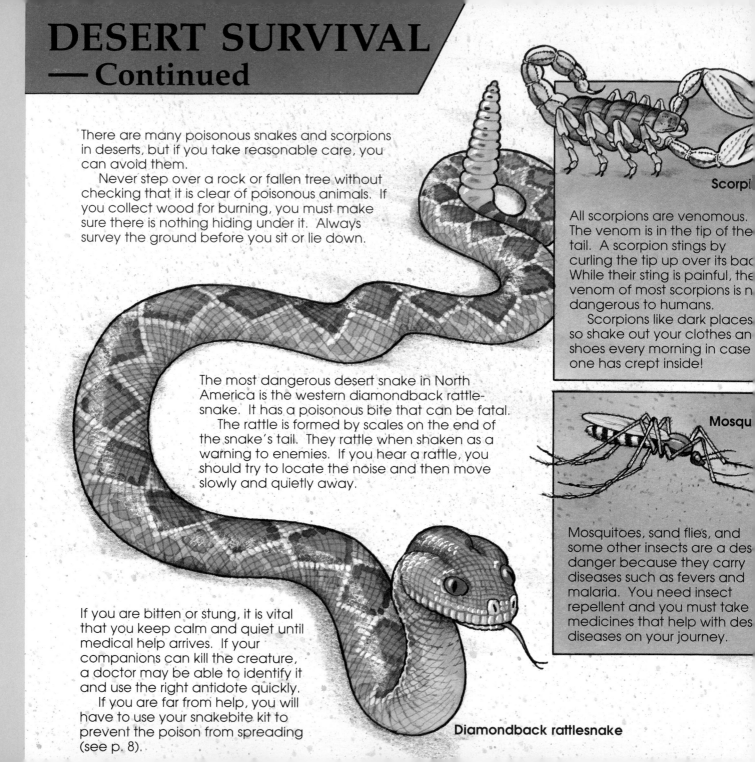

There are many poisonous snakes and scorpions in deserts, but if you take reasonable care, you can avoid them.

Never step over a rock or fallen tree without checking that it is clear of poisonous animals. If you collect wood for burning, you must make sure there is nothing hiding under it. Always survey the ground before you sit or lie down.

The most dangerous desert snake in North America is the western diamondback rattlesnake. It has a poisonous bite that can be fatal.

The rattle is formed by scales on the end of the snake's tail. They rattle when shaken as a warning to enemies. If you hear a rattle, you should try to locate the noise and then move slowly and quietly away.

If you are bitten or stung, it is vital that you keep calm and quiet until medical help arrives. If your companions can kill the creature, a doctor may be able to identify it and use the right antidote quickly.

If you are far from help, you will have to use your snakebite kit to prevent the poison from spreading (see p. 8).

Diamondback rattlesnake

Scorpi

All scorpions are venomous. The venom is in the tip of the tail. A scorpion stings by curling the tip up over its bac While their sting is painful, the venom of most scorpions is n dangerous to humans.

Scorpions like dark places so shake out your clothes an shoes every morning in case one has crept inside!

Mosqu

Mosquitoes, sand flies, and some other insects are a des danger because they carry diseases such as fevers and malaria. You need insect repellent and you must take medicines that help with des diseases on your journey.

Hyena

In Africa, you must be careful to not camp in places where domestic animals have been kept. Bushes, laid in a circle to keep the animals in, outline their paddock. The area may be infested with ticks that carry dangerous diseases.

It is unlikely that you will encounter many dangerous animals on a desert journey, but in many parts of Africa south of the Sahara, you might find lions, leopards, and hyenas. Stay out of their way!

Desert travelers sometimes see mirages, caused by layers of air of different temperatures bending light rays in unusual ways.

When this happens, the air shimmers and shines. It can look just like a lake in the middle of the desert! Mirages can also make distances appear much shorter than they really are.

Sometimes fast winds blow across the dry land, whipping up sand and dust into a sandstorm. If you see the horizon darken and an obvious haze of dust approaching, you must act quickly, closing vehicle windows and air intakes. If you are walking with a camel, you must make it lie down. Cover your face and sit, not lie, down until the storm subsides.

When the dust cloud reaches you, it will blot out the Sun. When it has passed, sand dunes may have moved or changed shape, and roads may be buried. You'll need to check your compass to decide which way to go.

13

DESERT MAMMALS

Animal bodies are mostly water — no creature could survive without it. In the desert, the problem for all animals is to find a water source, but many have adapted to cope with the drought conditions.

There is hardly any water on the desert surface and rain rarely falls. Animals have to get moisture by eating plants or other creatures. The best-known desert animal is the camel, which grazes on plants.

Camels are perfectly adapted for life in the desert. They can live for many days without water. Their wide, padded, webbed feet prevent them from sinking into soft sand, and their nostrils can close to keep out sand and dust.

Nostrils closed to keep out sand

Foot adapted for walking on sand

The Bactrian camel, which has two humps, still lives wild in the Gobi Desert of Central Asia. The dromedary, a one-humped camel, is a domestic working animal.

Mammals live in most deserts. For example, the bighorn sheep lives in scorching Death Valley in California.

In July, the temperature often reaches 125°F (52°C). Few animals can survive this intense heat. But the bighorn stores water in its stomach and can live off dry food for days.

Most desert animals keep out of the Sun. For example, the Arabian oryx shelters under rocks or trees in the daytime and feeds in the evening. Sometimes it scrapes a hole in the ground to sit on cool sand under the surface.

The ground squirrel of Africa's Kalahari Desert has feet padded with hair to protect them from the sand's heat.

It uses its long bushy tail as an umbrella over its head to shelter it from the Sun.

The Saharan fennec fox spends much of its day in a rock crevice or burrow, away from the heat. At night, it comes out to hunt for gerbils and other small animals. It has large triangular ears which pick up sounds well.

Big ears help to keep many desert animals cool and to stop them from losing too much water through sweat evaporating. The ears are covered with tiny blood vessels. As air blows across them, it cools the blood inside, helping to keep the animal's temperature down.

15

DESERT REPTILES

There are many types of desert snakes and lizards. These animals are reptiles, which means that they are cold-blooded. They cannot make their own body heat. Instead, the heat around them warms their bodies. When the weather is warm, they are active, but when it is cool, they must rest.

Desert snakes eat small animals such as rodents. Rattlesnakes and asps kill their prey by biting them and injecting them with poison, while snakes such as boas and pythons wrap around their victim and suffocate it.

Some desert snakes have developed a sidewinding movement to get good traction on soft sand. A sidewinding snake will arch the front part of its body and throw its head across the sand, pulling the rest of its body after it. In this way, it seems to roll sideways, leaving a trail of wavering lines behind.

Sand tracks

A sidewinding snake

Gila monster

The Gila monster and the beaded lizard of Mexico look alike and are the world's only venomous lizards. The Gila monster of the southern U.S. can grow up to 20 inches (51 cm) long. It eats insects and birds with its strong jaw and sharp teeth. When it bites its victim, poison trickles down grooves in its teeth into the wound.

During the heat of the day, the desert tortoises of North America hide in large, underground holes. In the early evening when the air is cooler, they slowly lumber from this chamber to munch on their favorite food, cacti. When a tortoise eats a cactus, tearing the plant into pieces with its horny bill, it stores the water from the plant in sacs under its shell.

The moloch lizard of the Australian desert has another name — the thorny devil. This is because its back is covered with spines that protect it against attacks from predators.

The moloch feeds on ants, sitting beside ant trails and lapping up the ants with its long tongue. It also has an unusual way of getting water — it seems to be able to absorb water from the air onto its skin. The water trickles down tiny grooves in the skin until it reaches the lizard's mouth.

Desert skinks are small lizards that have developed clever ways of moving underneath the surface of the sand to protect themselves from the Sun's heat.

Certain kinds of skinks living in African and Asian deserts are called sandfish. With their legs held close to their body, they seem to swim through the sand, hunting for beetles and millipedes.

Desert toads are amphibious, which means they can live on land or in water. One of the strangest desert amphibians is the spadefoot toad. It has powerful legs that it uses for burrowing into the desert soil in its native Nevada.

During hot spells, the toad stays buried in the soil for weeks or months at a time. It lines its burrow with a gelatin-like substance that helps it preserve the water in its body.

DESERT SPIDERS, INSECTS, AND BIRDS

Many insects and spiders live in the desert. Few desert spiders use webs to trap their prey — there are few plants for them to hang webs on and few flying insects to trap. Instead, the spiders hunt for their food on the ground.

The red-kneed tarantula is a hunting spider that lives in the deserts of Mexico and the southwestern United States. Its body is thickly covered with hairs that can pick up vibrations in the air and on the ground, telling it where prey may be found.

Tarantulas eat large insects, small animals, and other spiders.

The darkling beetle of the Sahara Desert has no wings. Instead, its outer wing cases are fused together, leaving a pocket of air underneath that protects the beetle from the heat of the Sun.

The tarantula hawk wasp hunts tarantulas. It stings and paralyzes the huge spiders and drags them to its burrow.

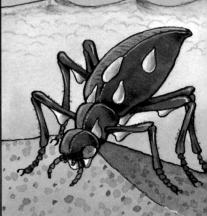

The ant lion is the larva of a fly found in the deserts of the United States. It catches its food by digging a pit in the sand and hiding in the bottom.

When an ant or other insect tumbles into the pit, the ant lion seizes it with its jaws. If the insect struggles free, the ant lion throws sand at its victim to make it fall back into the pit.

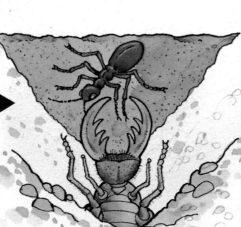

A different type of darkling beetle lives in the African Namib Desert, where clouds of fog roll in from the nearby South Atlantic Ocean. To get water, the beetle stands on top of a dune. The fog condenses into water on its body and the water drips into its mouth.

A few bird species live in the desert too! You can sometimes find birds hiding from the scorching daytime heat beneath plants or rocks. Their feathers are often puffed out to act as a barrier against the heat.

The ostrich is the largest bird in the world, growing as tall as 10 feet (3 m). It eats plants, small animals, and even sand, which helps the ostrich digest its food.

Like all desert animals, birds must get a supply of water. The African sand grouse even manages to carry water to its young. It flies to a pool and soaks up moisture in its breast feathers. Then it returns to its nest, where the chicks suck the water from the feathers.

Ostriches are commonly thought to bury their heads in sand. In reality, an ostrich will lower its head to the ground to avoid danger — it just looks as though its head has disappeared.

Roadrunners live in the deserts of Mexico and Arizona. They are famous for being fast, and with their strong legs, they can race at speeds of up to 15 miles (24 km) an hour.

The roadrunner feeds mainly on insects, lizards, and snakes. It can even tackle a rattlesnake, stabbing its prey with its sharp, strong bill and then swallowing the snake headfirst.

DESERT PLANTS

Plants are not rare in deserts. There is a surprising range of species growing in the dry areas of the world.

Desert plants gather water through their roots. The plants either spread out their roots near the surface to catch rain and dew or send them deep down to moist soil layers.

Water can evaporate through plant leaves. To conserve water, the desert cacti have no leaves at all.

Some succulent plants have thick fleshy leaves and stems to store water. These stems and leaves also have waterproof coverings to stop moisture from evaporating.

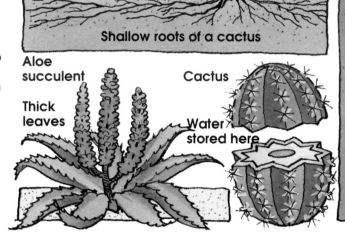

Shallow roots of a cactus

Aloe succulent

Thick leaves

Cactus

Water stored here

Deep roots of a eucalyptus

Cacti are well adapted for desert life. Some of them have pleats that can stretch out when a cactus takes in water and close up again as the water is used up.

Cacti often have spines or a bad taste to repel hungry animals. The spines can be large, so you must never try to push your way through a clump of them. If a large spine sticks to you, don't try to pull it off with your fingers because it might stick into your hand. It is better to use a comb to flick it off.

Perhaps the most spectacular desert plant is the saguaro cactus of the southwestern United States. It can grow up to 50 feet (15 m) high, with roots stretching out 35 feet (11 m) or more below the ground. The plants grow so close together in some areas that they look like a forest of trees.

The saguaro is home to the Gila woodpecker, which digs holes in the fleshy trunk. The elf owl, one of the smallest owls in the world, uses this hole for its nest. This bird is about the size of a sparrow.

Mojave Desert, California, after rain

Cacti are perennials, which means that they live for many years and can survive seasons with little rain. But some desert plants called ephemerals avoid droughts by growing, flowering, and seeding themselves only when the rains come. Their seeds can then survive for many years until the next rain falls.

Many ephemerals have beautiful flowers that only appear briefly after rain. Desert insects also hatch from their eggs when the rains come. Because the flowers don't live very long, they must attract the pollinating insects quickly, so they produce brightly colored blooms to lure these insects.

There are many types of desert trees. The biggest is the baobab, native to tropical Africa and now grown in other tropical countries. The baobab has the thickest trunk of any tree — it can grow up to 30 feet (9 m) in diameter! Since it can store a lot of water, it is especially suited to dry areas. You could get emergency water supplies by splitting open the spongy lower branches.

Baobab tree

DESERT PEOPLE

Many desert people are nomads, living in small family groups and moving from place to place in search of food. They often have livestock, such as goats, that graze on any plants they come across.

There are several different tribes living in the Sahara. One tribe consists of the tall Tuareg nomads from Algeria, Mali, and Niger.

The Tuareg breed camels and lead them in groups called caravans across the Sahara. They carry goods such as cloth, dates, and grains to major trading centers like Timbuktu.

Tuareg men often wear long blue and white robes. On their head, they wear a turban with a long cloth that can be pulled over the nose and mouth to keep out sand during desert windstorms.

Tuareg tents are portable and are usually made from leather over wooden frames carved with simple decorations. A gap around the bottom of the tent allows air to circulate. Sometimes, sticks are stuck around the outside to protect the tent from large animals.

If you visited the Tuareg, you would probably be offered tea to drink. They brew the tea in a careful ceremony. The Tuareg pour the hot green tea, mixed with sugar and mint, back and forth between two pots until it tastes just right. Everyone is expected to have three cupfuls, and to refuse is thought rude.

The Bedouin people of the Arabian Desert are like the Tuareg in some ways. They have the same religion, Islam, and travel the desert with their camels, sheep, and goats.

Bedouins make their tents from woolen strips of goat hair sewn together. Tall poles in the middle and short poles at the sides support the tent.

The Bedouins can tie down the side flaps to keep out dust and the glare of the Sun or tie them back to let in a cooling breeze.

There is no furniture inside a Bedouin tent. Instead, the occupants sit on cushions and colored rugs they have woven.

In one area of the tent, there is usually a charcoal fire burning in a hollow in the ground. The Bedouins hang woven flaps from the roof to divide the tent into rooms.

Many of today's Bedouin tribespeople are now selling their camels and buying trucks instead. They can use them to carry sheep and goats more quickly to new pastures, and it is much easier and quicker for them to drive their animals across the desert to local markets.

DESERT PEOPLE
—Continued

The San tribes of the African Kalahari Desert do not keep herds of animals or grow crops. Instead, they live off the food they find in the desert, gathering plants and hunting animals.

San huts are made with local materials. They have strong branches as a framework and a thatch of long grass.

Just outside their huts, the San usually light a fire using a wooden firestick. They place the firestick's pointed end into a notch cut in another stick, and spin the firestick between their hands. After a while, the wood dust catches fire and falls onto a wad of dry grass. Then dry sticks are piled on top.

The San are expert trackers and hunters. They make arrows and spears to kill animals such as antelope in the same way as people did in prehistoric times. They make the animal skins into clothing.

The women of a San village spend their day collecting plants for food. When water is scarce, they search for tuber roots. They scrape the tubers into a pulp and squeeze the liquid out.

The San find the water they need at tiny water holes in the desert. They suck the water up through hollow sticks and transfer it to ostrich eggshells for storage.

24

The Aboriginals have lived in the Australian Outback for at least 40,000 years. Settlers have taken much of their land and many Aboriginals have moved to the cities or work on ranches. But there are still a few tribes living in the old way.

The Aboriginals are adept at using the things around them. They build their shelters from poles and eucalyptus bark and they weave belts, fishing lines, and baskets out of string made from a bark fiber.

Aboriginals are able to live in the harsh Outback by trekking in search of animals and water. They know where and when food can be found and are expert trackers, hunting animals such as kangaroos, emus, and wombats.

When there is no big game to be found, the Aboriginals catch lizards, frogs, and turtles to eat, or they dig in the ground for ants or grubs. The ants taste rather like honey and the grubs taste like nuts.

Aboriginal tribal groups follow desert paths they believe were taken by their ancestors long ago in the Dreamtime — a legendary period when the world began.

The Aboriginals believe that the beings of Dreamtime have left signs of their presence in rocks, plants, and animals.

DESERT MYSTERIES

There are many natural desert puzzles worth solving, such as how animals adapt to desert life and how plants can survive for years with no water. There are also some strange and dramatic mysteries that you might be lucky enough to come across, and perhaps even solve, on a desert journey.

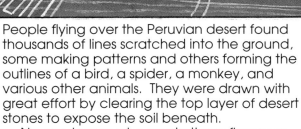

In 1876, the German explorer Erwin von Bary found crocodile tracks in the middle of the Sahara, one of the driest areas of the world. For a long time, almost no one believed him, until 1908, when a hunter shot a crocodile.

People think there are still isolated crocodile groups living in small pools in the heart of the Sahara, although no one knows how they got there!

People flying over the Peruvian desert found thousands of lines scratched into the ground, some making patterns and others forming the outlines of a bird, a spider, a monkey, and various other animals. They were drawn with great effort by clearing the top layer of desert stones to expose the soil beneath.

No one knows who made these figures or why. Some people think they are a giant calendar or a religious monument.

In the late 1800s, Jacob Waltz, a German immigrant, disappeared into the Superstition Mountains of the Arizona desert and returned with gold! He repeated his trip many times, and reputedly found over $300,000 worth of treasure.

Waltz, often called "the Dutchman," died in Phoenix in 1891 without ever revealing the location of his mine. Many people have searched for it since. No one has ever found the "Lost Dutchman Mine," but several people have died trying.

One of the commonest desert mysteries is how news travels so rapidly. For example, you might be sitting in a tent alone in the Kalahari when suddenly a San tribesman will appear, having walked several miles to meet you.

If you asked your visitor how he knew you were there, he would probably say that he had heard, even though you may not have seen or spoken to anyone for many days. How does this happen? Some people think it is telepathy but no one really knows.

On the arid plateau of Tassili n'Ajjer in the Sahara are some beautiful rock paintings that show that the desert was once rich with animals and plants. There are pictures of antelope, goats, sheep, cattle, and even elephants.

Very little is known about the people who painted these mysterious pictures, but they certainly lived in a very different Sahara from the one we see today. No one knows why the pictures were painted or how they have survived the wind and Sun for so long.

27

DESERT FUTURE

The deserts of the world are changing quickly. People are now increasingly developing them. But this development can do great harm if it is not planned properly. We must do careful scientific studies to prevent damage to this sometimes fragile environment.

Food crops can be grown in desert regions if the ground is irrigated, which means it is supplied with water through pipe systems and channels.

There are many new projects for desert irrigation around the world. But they all need careful planning or they could destroy the desert soil instead of improving it.

People are examining deserts to see whether they can produce useful products without irrigation. For example, researchers are analyzing native plants to see if any of them can produce chemicals or animal food.

Farmers have already cultivated one desert plant, the jojoba bush, which can produce oil that can be used for many different products, such as cosmetics and hair shampoo.

If desert people could cultivate their crops for profit, they might be able to obtain better food supplies and a higher standard of living. Unless scientists can help them do this, many may move away from the desert cities and their ancient cultures could die out.

In some desert areas, plant life is gradually being destroyed as animals overgraze the land. Eventually, the soil itself is eroded by wind and rain, and land bordering the over-grazed desert becomes overwhelmed by wind-blown sand.

This process is called desertification. Combined with bad farming practices and drought, desertification has resulted in the loss of millions of square miles of farmland.

The deserts formed in this way are barren and ugly. One example is the Sahel region, south of the Sahara. A few years ago, a long drought dried up the soil and killed the plants. This resulted in the Sahara Desert moving south by many miles. Scientists are trying to slow down the desertification process.

We are not sure whether deserts will remain full of interesting wildlife or whether they will increasingly become barren wastelands where no creatures can survive, where the desert plants are destroyed and the soil eroded away.

By learning as much as we can about deserts, we may be able to prevent damage by humans and save the animals, plants, and people who make the deserts their home.

FOR MORE INFORMATION

Magazines

Here are some children's magazines that may have articles about the world's deserts and the wildlife that lives there. If your library or bookstore does not have them, write to the publishers listed below for information about subscribing.

Audubon Adventure
National Audubon Society
950 Third Avenue
New York, NY 10022

Dodo Dispatch
34th Street and Girard
Philadelphia, PA 19104

Elsa's Echo
3201 Tepusquet Canyon
Santa Maria, CA 93454

Owl
The Young Naturalist Foundation
59 Front Street East
Toronto, Ontario
Canada M5E 1B3

National Geographic World
National Geographic Society
17th and M Streets NW
Washington, DC 20036

Ranger Rick
National Wildlife Federation
1412 16th Street NW
Washington, DC 20036

3-2-1 Contact
Children's Television Workshop
One Lincoln Plaza
New York, NY 10023

Tracks
P.O. Box 30235
Lansing, MI 48909

Addresses

The organizations listed below have information about deserts and the plant and animal species living there. When you write to them, tell them exactly what you want to know.

California Native Plant Society
909 12th Street, Suite 116
Sacramento, CA 95814

Desert Botanical Garden
1201 North Galvin Parkway
Phoenix, AZ 85008

Books

The following books concern deserts and the people, plants, and animals that live there. If you are not able to find them in your library or bookstore, ask someone to order them for you.

Animals of the Deserts. Johnson (Lerner)
Cactus. Overbeck (Lerner)
Deserts. Goetz (William Morrow)
Deserts. Wilkes (EDC)
Deserts and People. Carson (Silver Burdett)
Deserts and Wastelands. Dixon
   (Franklin Watts)

The Gentle Desert: Exploring an Ecosystem. Pringle
   (Macmillan)
Life on a Giant Cactus. Lauber (Garrard)
A Look at the Earth Around Us: Deserts.
   (National Geographic Society)
Red Earth, Blue Sky: The Australian Outback. Rau
   (Crowell)

Glossary

Bactrian
A camel with two humps on its back that lives in the Gobi Desert in Asia. With its thick winter fleece, the Bactrian camel is well suited to cold climates. Nomads use the Bactrian as a beast of burden.

Caravan
A company of travelers journeying together, especially across a desert. Camel caravans can cover 20-25 miles (32-40 km) in one day.

Desertification
The process of changing once fertile land into a desert. This process often begins when hillside trees are cut down for fields or firewood. Plowing then breaks up the soil and rain washes it down the slope. When the land can no longer support crops, many animals overgraze the remaining plants. More soil is washed or blown away, leaving bare rock.

Dreamtime
A time when the Aboriginal people of Australia believe the world began. Aboriginals base their myths in this time long ago when humans supposedly were the only living animals on Earth. When disasters shook the Earth, some of these people transformed themselves into birds, plants, animals, insects, and even rocks in an attempt to hide and protect themselves. The remaining people developed rituals, paintings, and other ways of honoring their changed relatives.

Dromedary
A camel with one hump that lives in North Africa and the Middle East. It is also known as the Arabian camel. Like *Bactrians*, they will eat almost any kind of dry plant. When food is abundant, a camel stores energy in the form of fat in its hump — not water, as many people believe. Camels can drink 20 gallons (76 liters) of water in 10 minutes and up to 50 gallons (190 liters) in a day!

Ephemerals
Plants with a short life cycle.

Oryx
An antelope with straight or slightly back-curved horns and a light-colored coat. Oryx can tolerate temperatures up to 104°F (40°C) without losing much water.

Perennials
Plants that have a life span of more than two years. Many perennials store the nourishment they require for rapid growth in their bulbs, stems, and *tubers*.

Rain Shadow
An area on the sheltered, or leeward, side of a mountain range where there is usually less rainfall than on the other, windward, side. A rain shadow is most likely to occur in regions where a large mountain range lies at a right angle to the usual direction of winds and storms.

Succulents
Plants with thick, fleshy leaves or stems that conserve moisture.

Telepathy
A way of transferring thoughts from one person to another without using speech, touch, taste, sight, or sound. Researchers are not sure that telepathy is actually possible. Some people think that since thought is a form of energy that produces electrical impulses, these impulses could travel from one person to another under certain conditions.

Tuber
An underground part of certain plants. The plant uses the tuber to store food and as a way to reproduce. Perhaps the best-known tuber is the potato.

Venoms
Deadly or poisonous substances produced by animals. Some animals can inject the venom through wounds that they make in their victims. Others have venom glands and ducts but no way to inject the poison. Animals use venom both to catch prey and for self-defense.

Index